CREATING A HOME FOR LEARNING: THE ART AND SCIENCE OF TEACHING

A SURVIVAL GUIDE TO THE CLASSROOM

BY

JIM SLOUFFMAN
AND
RYAN HALL

ISBN: 1-4107-0945-0 (e-book)
ISBN: 1-4107-0946-9 (Paperback)
ISBN: 1-4107-0947-7 (Hardcover)

Library of Congress Control Number: 2002096918

This book is printed on acid free paper.

Printed in the United States of America
Bloomington, IN

1stBooks - rev. 03/07/03

This book is dedicated to our students who come to us needful and deserving of compassion.

The authors of this book would like to thank the following people for their assistance and guidance through our publication process: Mary Ann Davis, Vicky Mary, Teresa Meyer, Sharon Obermeyer, Sandy Robinson, and Chas. E. Martin.

The authors would also like to thank their wonderful wives, Carolann Slouffman and Stephanie Hall, for their unconditional support and advice. Further, their unwavering belief in the goodness of our project was not only much appreciated, but needed as well.

Table of Contents

"There is neither a painting in the mind nor a mind in the painting;

and yet, where else can one find a painting than in the mind?"

-Buddha

Introduction

"Reality is what we take to be true. What we take to be true is what we believe. What we believe is based upon our perceptions. What we perceive depends on what we look for. What we look for depends on what we think. What we think depends on what we perceive. What we perceive determines what we believe. What we believe determines what we take to be true. What we take to be true is our reality."

- David Bohm, physicist

Creating a Home for Learning: The Art and Science of Teaching is designed to be a survival guide to the classroom. It seeks to address the inner-thought processes involved in teaching as well as the interpersonal and organizational skills that support a *heart-centered approach*. When you choose to adopt this approach toward your classroom, a myriad of delightful happenings start to manifest in the teaching environment.

The first thing that one notices in the classroom is the warm feelings that start to permeate the environment, replacing feelings of fear and anxiety. Smiles start to replace scowls and eyes start to brighten and make contact where before contact was sadly absent. This *heart-centered approach* to teaching yields greater productivity because the best outcome derives from what is best for the students, which is what is best for the class/family as a whole. This sense of community in the classroom provides support to each class/family member and can significantly reduce stress, as a sense of well-being and interdependence starts to emerge. Less stress on the group yields bonding. A more bonded group can provide more growth for the individual. *This is the goal of all teaching.*

"It is essential to enjoy the conditions of teaching, to feel at home in a room containing twenty healthy young people, and to make our enjoyment of this group-feeling give us energy for our teaching."
- Gilbert Highet, American classicist

The *Art of Teaching* explores the inner thought process involved in teaching and why it is so important to creating a home for learning. My old grade school basketball coach used to make us repeat before every important game, "Where is the game? It's in your head!" Similarly, your vision influences your ability to create a home for learning. We will explore ways of creating a functional home/family in your classroom and look at the symbolic significance of our traditional final outcome, graduation. Finally, we will ponder how profoundly teachers impact an individual's life and what it means to our greater community.

The *Science of Teaching* explores the interpersonal and organizational skills that are so important in being successful in the classroom. This section also delves into staying organized and providing the most efficient delivery system possible for your lessons. In these chapters you will gain the confidence necessary to maintain that all-important comfort zone that is needed to perpetuate a heart-centered approach to teaching.

This book is filled with examples of student success stories, anecdotes, famous quotes and wisdoms gained through years of classroom and corporate training experiences that Jim Slouffman and Ryan Hall have had over the years. It also includes some workshop-type learning activities that will enable you to experience this heart-centered and practical approach to teaching. Most importantly, it seeks to be a guide that will once again make teaching the joyful and noble profession that it was always meant to be.

Teaching is a service profession and is essential to the survival and maintenance of our world community. What better way to serve than through using a *heart-centered and effective approach to teaching!*

"*One thing I know: The only ones among you who will really be happy are those who will have sought and found how to serve.*"
-Dr. Albert Schweitzer, German philosopher and philanthropist

Chapter 1 – Creating a Home for Learning

"A happy person promotes a happy home. A happy home promotes a happy neighborhood. Such a neighborhood affects a city, which in turn inspires a state. A happy state touches a nation. A happy nation helps create a happy world. So being a happy person is the most important thing in the world."

-Sally Hess, Caring citizen

Creating a functional home/family for learning

What does a classroom and a home have in common? Let's just think about that for a minute. They both provide a space in which people dwell for a period of time. People derive nourishment from each environment, be it intellectual or physical. Both places can be comforting and a shelter from the disturbances of the world outside. In all cultures, home and hearth are central to our concept of family and community.

In today's modern society, family has undergone immense change. Support that was traditionally being provided by families is now being provided by teachers in educational institutions. In a society that continually struggles with challenges of violence and crime, the levels of social functionality are always in question. Recent cross-cultural studies have revealed that around 80 percent of families in this country are dysfunctional. Communication breakdowns, lack of support for individual family members and feelings of disconnectedness permeate these kinds of families. About 50 percent of first marriages end in divorce and most children in America grow up in single-parent or blended families. If this describes the environment of most homes in our community it also describes the environment of most classrooms and your home for learning.

Our classrooms are really a smaller and somewhat shorter stay version of the homes that we provide for our families. So in essence, our classrooms are a home for learning. If we view this home for learning with the same perspective as family members coming together once or twice a week for a learning visit, we change our attitude toward teaching considerably. If in fact we treat our students with the same respectful caring that we treat our closest relatives, at least the relatives we like, then a whole world of educational possibilities start to surface. Think of your classroom as a home for learning. You provide the structure and parenting, and together with your students, you form a functional family.

"A teacher is a child's third parent."
                                -Hyman Maxwell Berston, American educator

This caring approach we call *heart-centered teaching*. This approach is critical to creating a home for learning. Once you have adopted the heart-centered approach to teaching, amazing things will start to happen in your classroom. Students will feel more comfortable in class. They will start helping one another reach class goals as they form tighter bonds with one another. Additionally, some of these bonds will last a lifetime. A functional home will be experienced for perhaps the first time in some students' lives. The more secure your educational family becomes the more learning will be increased and the more learning is increased the more teacher satisfaction is gained. What a win-win situation for all involved!

So how do we as educators nurture *a heart-centered approach* to teaching? The place to start is by taking a long look at how we as teachers impact the lives of our students. A truly *heart-centered* teacher is fully aware of the effect they have on the lives of those present in their home for learning. This empowerment can only lead to a *heart-centered approach* and the truly personal rewards gained from working in a home for learning.

Let us next examine the impact of teachers as mentors on our own lives and start to get in touch with our inner feelings about *heart-centered* teaching.

> *"Actions speak louder than words; let your words teach and your actions speak."*
>
> - Saint Anthony of Padua, Portuguese Franciscan monk

Teachers as mentors

Teachers impact the lives of their students in much the same way that parents impact the lives of their children. The main difference here being that of quality-growth time versus life-long guidance time. In a brief focus of class time, teachers with the ability to act as mentors can have a lasting impact on students. How did we learn our initial set of life skills? It was our parents who were our original mentors. Our teachers became our mentors for most of our primary, secondary and advanced life skill sets. The key to being a successful mentor lies in the heart of the teacher and what the heart projects.

Reflect on your life for a moment and identify a teacher who acted as a mentor to you. Take a few moments and reflect on this notion and write your thoughts below, describing how this individual impacted your life.

_____

_____

_____

_____

_____

_____

_____

_____

_____

_____

_____

_____

_____

Next, think about the symbolic meaning of graduation and how it relates to mentoring students. Graduation represents the rite of passage from being a student to living a transformed life. The degree, diploma, or certificate empowers the now successful individual to use his or her newly developed skills and knowledge as a productive citizen.

I am reminded of a situation that happened at a graduation a few years back. Graduation being my favorite moment as an educator, I am often found circulating through the crowded lobby of the auditorium just prior to the start of the ceremony. I take great delight in seeing the families proudly gathering about their special graduate in support. Moments like these reinforce my strong beliefs in what a home for learning can truly produce.

One evening as I was conducting my usual walk about, I spotted a rather unusual sight over in the corner of the lobby. It was Tim, one of my students, surrounded by his family - his mom and dad, sisters and brothers, grandparents and an aunt and uncle. Tim had a difficult life prior to attending our college. Problems with drugs, alcohol and the law had plagued him throughout high school. He was desperately seeking to turn his troubled life around. Everything appeared normal until I got a little closer to the family huddled in the corner. However, the part of this scene that disturbed me was that some of them were crying. Astonished by this emotional outburst, I decided to investigate. I asked Tim if there was some kind of problem and if I could be of any assistance. Tim dried his tears and replied as follows: "Not to worry, Mr. Slouffman. You see, we are just happy because I am the first one in our entire family to have ever graduated from college! These are tears of joy because at last we have this success to share."

Well, the look in all of their eyes told the whole story. There was a look of pride and accomplishment in the adults, a look of hope and anticipation in the children and a look of confidence and joy in Tim. How many future generations of Tim's family will be affected by this moment of transformation?

"One good teacher in a lifetime may sometimes change a delinquent into a solid citizen."
-Philip Wylle, American writer

Teachers as mentors play a major role in the transformation of student to graduate and to lead successful lives. To witness this symbolic rite of passage is truly a teacher's finest hour. The ripple effect from this transformation travels through a myriad of lives, and eventually, impacts the community, nation, and world in which we live.

Let us proclaim the **NOBLE VIRTUE OF THE EDUCATOR** to be: "You change people's lives, therefore, you transform the world."

This transformation has a lasting and powerful impact on our society. As heart-centered teachers we have the ability to transform our students, their families, the businesses they will go to work for and our nation as a whole.

To appreciate the educator's role, we can look at the word *transform* and how it might relate to our students. The dictionary describes 'transform' as follows: *1. to change in structure, appearance, or character 2. change in potential or type.* This is what Tim and his family were celebrating.

Be a *heart-centered* teacher who creates a home for learning in the classroom and actively participate in transforming lives for the better!

Teachers are Wizards

Empower yourself with the following image – *"Teachers are Wizards."* In the legend of King Arthur, Merlin was a mentor to Arthur by helping him to realize his inner potential. Helping students find and access their inner assets is one of the most rewarding aspects of the *heart-centered approach* to teaching.

> *"I do not believe that we can put into anyone ideas which are not in him already."*
> -Dr. Albert Schweitzer, German philosopher and philanthropist

The Wizard of Oz is another example from myth of a heart-centered and inspired teacher. At the point of transformation when the Wizard bestowed upon the four travelers outward symbols of what they had been searching for, the Wizard simply revealed to them that what they were seeking, was held inside themselves all along. On their long journey, the yellow brick road provided each of the travelers with a set of challenges to overcome. As each obstacle was faced and overcome, each traveler grew in confidence and self-esteem. Even though darkness and fear were around every corner, this bonded little family of individuals worked toward reaching their final goal. The Emerald City was thought to be the ultimate destination for solving their problems, but proved to be a gateway to the inner-realization of their own strengths. The Wizard had only to present each traveler with an outward symbol of what they had already realized deep inside. Educators need to be the wizards that facilitate the path leading students to the realization of their inner potential.

Conclusion

Like the great artist Michelangelo who could see the form of his sculpture present in the uncut stone, our students are mere diamonds in the rough waiting to be revealed.

Be an inspired and *heart-centered* teacher! Accept the following professional challenge and provide your students with:

- **Brains =**   **Knowledge/Skills =**   **Scarecrow**
- **Courage =**   **Self-Esteem =**   **Lion**

- **Heart =**   **Desire to Succeed =**   **Tin Man**
- **Home =**   **Home for Learning =**   **Dorothy**

If you empower yourself with the noble virtue of the educator using a mentoring style that incorporates both the *Art and Science of Teaching*, then you will find your way into the inner reality of *heart-centered* teaching.

"Know thyself."
      -Inscription on the Temple of Apollo at Delphi

Chapter 2 – The Art of Teaching

"The art of teaching is the art of assisting discovery."
-Mark Van Doren, American poet and editor

Now that you have realized the importance of taking a *heart–centered approach* to teaching, we can now concentrate on some time-tested practical applications that will help increase your effectiveness in your home for learning. Quality teaching is both "an art and a science." The "science" involves skills of program planning and development, instructional planning, execution and evaluation, and instructional management. These are the essential building blocks to build your home for learning. We will further explore these subjects in chapter three.

Teaching is also an "art." These skills, behaviors, and personal characteristics, which will be explored in this chapter, are the mortar that holds the building blocks together and provides the foundation for your home for learning.

Creating a caring environment

The greatest obstacle to overcome in creating a strong home for learning is fear. Remember back to your first day of class in kindergarten or first grade. I don't know about you, but I, for one, was petrified! The smells of the classroom were new and foreign. It must have been that white glue paste and construction paper. The students' faces were all new; some faces carried brilliant smiles, some were on the verge of tears. To say the least, it left a lasting psychological impression. A similar fear enters all of our students each time they enter our classroom for the first time. Being with all new people for the first time and feeling insecure or even lost at times can be horrifying. The home for learning is designed to eliminate a greater part of this fear by fostering a caring environment.

The home for learning is a caring environment. First impressions always leave lasting effects. Start your class on the first day by establishing a caring environment that helps eliminate fear in your students. Students are a lot like people! I know this is shocking, but it is true. They need to know that you care. To care is to create a nurturing environment in which students can grow as individuals. Consider the power of a smile or a word of encouragement placed at just the right moment. Caring which emanates from the heart is the quickest way to develop a nurturing environment in your classroom and to foster student trust. This will go far to help eliminate fear on that very important first day and beyond.

Take a few moments and identify ways to create a more caring environment for you and your students.

_____

_____

_____

_____

_____

_____

_____

_____

_____

_____

_____

_____

_____

_____

_____

_____

_____

_____

_____

_____

"Kids go where there is excitement. They stay where there is love."

— Zig Ziglar, American motivational speaker

So, what's love got to do with it?

I am constantly being asked this simple question, "How did you become a successful teacher?" While this is a very complex question and should be answered at great length, my response is always the same, "I love my students." This statement always produces an initial shock then an inquisitive request for an explanation. I start my explanation by saying that this love is structured in the framework of my classroom rules and curriculum structure. I further define this loving style as being the focal point of the heart-centered approach to teaching. A loving approach in the classroom creates the same feeling as a loving family does at home. So, you see, we are once again back to creating that home for learning in the classroom.

How many times do you remember when you were in school asking a fellow classmate or friend about a teacher that you were anticipating having in class or were just curious about their reputation? What is the usual response that you would get? I almost always replied, "I loved that teacher!" or "I hated that teacher." Which label would you desire to have attached to your name? Well, it is obvious that we all want to be loved. Let's do an analysis of why a teacher might be described as loved. The hated teacher we will call "A", the loved teacher will be referred to as "B."

First of all, as the old adage says, if you don't give any love, you don't get any love. By love I mean projecting a caring attitude in all of your interactions with your students. This could be a smile when the frustration over lack of accomplishment is at its peak. Perhaps it's helping a student approach a problem that they are seeking to solve by presenting them with another tool to use in solving that problem. Remember, nothing succeeds like success and in giving away a little success, a student may gain the confidence to achieve even more.

I am reminded of a student that I once had in a color theory class who was becoming greatly frustrated by a production problem that she just could not solve. Of course, the usual response to this frustrating situation is: "I can't do it. I give up." There are two responses that can be delivered in this situation. Teacher "A" might respond in this fashion: "Well that is your problem. Figure it out on your own or you are going to flunk!"

Teacher "B" might respond in this fashion: "Let's take a look at what is going on with this challenge that you are having and see if we can improve the outcome."

Here are two responses and two very different impacts on the student. My response to my frustrated color theory student was similar to teacher "B." I helped the student gain a little success by redoing a demonstration and assisting the student in creating part of a solution to the problem. This led to a small feeling of accomplishment which translated into more confidence and the student turned around what would have been a failing course into a passing course. My caring/loving response will not be forgotten by this student or by the other class members that witnessed my approach. This effect spread throughout my home for learning and our little family went on to face our next challenge. Perhaps my love for my students is only a reflection of my love of teaching.

"One looks back with appreciation to the brilliant teachers, but with gratitude to those who touched our human feelings. The curriculum is so much necessary raw material, but warmth is the vital element for growing a plant and for the soul of the child."
                                                  -Carl Jung, Swiss psychiatrist

Take a few moments and think about a caring response that you received from a teacher in your past. Write down the feelings that you experienced when you knew that your teacher really cared.

_____

_____

_____

_____

_____

_____

_____

"My joy in learning is that it enables me to teach."
-Seneca, Roman writer and tutor

Motivating Learners

Motivating learners is one of the most challenging parts of teaching. Using grades to motivate students seems to be the most popular practice of our day. But what if it were supplemented by a healthy dose of teacher enthusiasm and responsiveness? *Enthusiasm in the classroom is the best way to energize and motivate your students.* A teacher's natural passion for their subject will keep students on task and focused no matter what challenge you may present them. How many times have you walked into a classroom or training session only to find a boring chalk and talk presentation that may have delivered the facts about a given subject, but promoted more sleep than enthusiasm? Your energy level in the home for

20

learning will directly effect your student's motivation. Always start with a bang and end on a reassuring note. Recap at the end of class what you have accomplished that day. It may even surprise you on occasion what all you and your group has gotten done together!

Utilizing stories from your professional work experience is a great way to motivate learners. For instance, describe how the skill being taught in your class has helped you solve a problem professionally. This creates a picture of the reality behind the theory of what you are presenting in the classroom. Bringing relevance to what the lesson or project is trying to achieve is also a motivating factor. Remember, students are a lot like people; they need to know why they are learning a particular concept or technique. Constantly bringing your lessons back to why they are important to the student's future is of great importance to maintaining a motivating environment. Enriching that lesson's relevance with positive stories from your own experiences will reinforce to the student that they have an exciting journey ahead.

Being responsive to students' needs is important to creating a caring environment. When students notice a teacher's willingness to respond to their needs, a teacher communicates a feeling of respect and equality in the home for learning. This feeling that everyone is working equally for the mutual benefit of the group motivates students to do their best on behalf of the group. Something that has always worked well for me is what I call constant name recognition. I will constantly ask the student how they are progressing in their studies by using their name in the questioning process. For example, I may see the same student three times in one day and I may recognize their name in three different ways. For instance: "Hi John, how are things going today?"; "John, are you staying caught up on last week's assignment?"; and "Hey John, good job on that quiz that you handed in last week!"

By using the student's name in each question/statement, I am personalizing my greeting and soliciting a personal response to my interaction. This, once again, reinforces to that student that I care about their progress and success. Students find this family-like feeling motivating and comfortable.

Recently, one of my students, Julie, approached me with a question about her graduation requirements. Julie had been a part-time student and it was taking her twice as long as other students to finish her program. Being a single parent with two children, she had other priorities to consider. As she was probing me about how long it would take to finish her studies, I sensed from her a feeling of frustration and fear that she would never finish. I realized that this situation presented a challenge to me as a teacher as well as a great opportunity. In a split second I seized the opportunity to make a difference in this student's life. I thought to myself-how might I take this situation and turn it into a motivational session at this critical moment? I responded with a little creative visualization.

I told Julie that while it looked like a long way off and a great challenge, we could work with her to achieve her goal. We sat down together and worked out a road map for how many quarters it would take her to graduate. We plotted out the sequence of courses left to take and discussed at length how wonderful it was going to be when she received her degree on graduation night. We laughed away any fears that she had and she took the little hand-written plan with her that day. At the end of our short 10 minute meeting, she had a smile on her face and was feeling good about reaching her goals. I realized that we had relinquished some of her fears and created a vision of success. I profoundly realized at that moment that I could have created a very different outcome if I had chosen to respond by saying, "Sorry, I don't have any time to discuss this with you today." You see, motivating students in a home for learning does have its responsibilities and priorities.

A few years later, Julie had finally made it to graduation night. She showed up with her children and her new husband. Everyone was excited about the big night. She pulled me aside at one point and told me that she had something to show me. She pulled out a tattered piece of paper and slowly unfolded it. It was our road map to success that we had written down a few years earlier. With tears in her eyes, she explained to me that she had kept that paper in her purse as a constant reminder that there was hope if she stayed focused on the road map to success. Julie just needed to know that someone else also believed that she could be successful. What a joyous moment for us both and what a wonderful example of why a home for learning is so very important. *Motivate your students by using a <u>heart-centered approach</u> to teaching, enhanced by enthusiasm and responsiveness.*

"I touch the future. I teach."
- Christa McAuliffe, American Teacher and Astronaut

Tough Caring

The home for learning is no different than any other home and sometimes it can be disrupted. Students can carry chips on their shoulders, have attitude challenges, and can harbor hard feelings for a number of reasons. What do you do when your classroom is disrupted by a student who refuses to cooperate with your instruction? Sometimes you have to respond with some *tough caring*. The home for learning is a nurturing environment filled with caring and support. It must, however, be maintained within the context of your policies and rules of conduct. This provides the structure by which you can maintain order and progress with your caring. An essential component of tough caring is communicating clearly your policies and rules of conduct. The best way to approach this is directly! Always publish your policies and hand them out to your students at the start of the quarter or semester. Explain the policies after handing them out and answer any question that the students may have about them. Continue to reinforce the positive aspects of the structure whenever a challenge to the structure occurs. By demonstrating how this structure benefits the whole group, students will see that it has their best interest at heart. Students, like children, like to know where the line is drawn in the sand. They want to know what their limitations are but need them to be communicated clearly and with respect.

When a confrontation does happen, what is the best way to handle it? Remember, the rule of thumb is to always be firm, but fair. It requires that you handle this difficult situation with grace and stay on purpose with a *heart-centered approach*. Tempers need to stay calm and even. If a student's temper explodes in my class, the very first thing that I do is stop what I am doing and shift my priority to resolving the situation that has arisen. Some situations just cannot wait until later! Next, without making any comments, I request a conference with the student outside of the classroom. This allows me the opportunity to discuss the student's behavior directly without the rest of the class observing and providing support to either side. Holding students fully responsible for their behavior is of utmost importance to maintaining the home for learning. Each member of the community must be responsible for their contribution, as well as how their behavior impacts the group. Often, students come to us in the mode of playing the blame game: "the teacher is the reason why I am doing poorly," or "the teacher doesn't like me and that's why my grades are so low." This is a carry-over from past educational experiences where limitations and responsibilities were not spelled out in advance or were used in an abusive manner. Being aware of the importance of tough caring in handling conflict resolution will provide you with a structure on which to build productive relationships in your home for learning.

I am reminded of a recent classroom situation where *tough caring* was of utmost importance to bringing resolution to a very tough circumstance. I was in the midst of my introductory lecture when I noticed a disturbance coming from the back of the classroom. Disturbances seem to always come from the back of the classroom. As you know, the introductory portion of any course is of utmost importance in establishing your command of the subject, as well as how you will set the tone for operating your home for learning. The way you respond to student questions and solve any challenges during class time speaks volumes to the students and the future time you will spend with them. It is critical time spent in support of where you are heading and a disturbance can create a train wreck effect if not handled properly. It is a moment of truth for your home for learning.

I noticed that one of my new students, Jeff, was holding a semi-loud conversation that had encircled several students in its grasp. From what I could hear, Jeff was informing the others of how my lecture was worthless and that, in his opinion, the subject that was being taught was a complete waste of everyone's time! This was preceded by note passing, laughter, and snickering. That should have been my first clue that something was brewing. Needless to say, I was not amused. Jeff was a student of many talents–not the least of which was that of great leadership ability. All of the students loved him, and because he was older than the majority of the class, he commanded their respect and was very popular. My first line of defense was to stop speaking for a moment or two, stare at the back of the room and wait until the disturbance came to an end. This worked momentarily, but soon the disturbance began again with renewed vigor. It was the critical moment for action. I stopped at the end of a topic break and asked my class to give me a moment. I asked Jeff to meet me in the hallway. Jeff slowly dragged himself away from his desk and made his way out of the room. When we made it to the end of the hallway it was just enough time for me to calm down and collect my thoughts a little. My first question for Jeff was why did he make the comments that he made. His response was that he felt that he already knew the subject through and through and this lecture was a waste of his time. I congratulated him on his complete mastering of our subject, but explained how his outburst had negatively impacted our group. I then explained our policy on class disturbances and discussed with him that he was responsible to maintain and adhere to the policy like everyone else. Jeff's response to my statement was that even though I had published my classroom standards and distributed them to the class, he did not agree with them and had his own beliefs and standards to follow. This was certainly getting sticky! I paused and responded in a calm voice that while everyone can choose their own beliefs, while present in my home for learning the environment was structured according to my published standards and rules. If he had a problem adhering to this structure he needed to withdraw from my class. I next advised Jeff to pack his things and leave class for the rest of the day and get back to me with his final decision as to whether he wanted to stay in the class or not. He packed his things with a scowl and promptly left the room. The class suddenly got very quiet and I finished the lecture and ended my class on an upbeat note.

Tough caring demands consistency in maintaining standards. Jeff's way of establishing his leadership in class was to create a confrontation with the teacher and see who backs down first. If he can achieve this during a lecture perhaps he can do the same thing on an important test. Jeff eventually decided to stay in class and his behavior did improve in time. He eventually dropped out of school and moved on to other things where his behavior continued to remain confrontational.

Conclusion

The home for learning has its limits and behaviors that are acceptable and some that are unacceptable. We teach by example as much as by our subject lessons and how you manage your group's behavior is critical to being successful. *Tough caring* has the betterment of the group's progress and well-being at the base of its values. Students like to know their limitations, but must have them communicated to them clearly.

"Teaching is painful, continual, and difficult work to be done by kindness, by watching and by praise, but above all by example."
- John Ruskin, British art critic

Try to think of an example of how you can use tough caring in a difficult classroom challenge. Write down a conflict or confrontation and then write a *tough caring* solution to that challenge. Remember, your base structure is your published standards and policies.

Conflict or Confrontation:

_____

_____

_____

_____

_____

_____

_____

_____

_____

Tough Caring Solution:

_____

_____

_____

_____

_____

_____

_____

_____

_____

_____

_____

_____

_____

_____

_____

_____

_____

_____

_____

_____

_____

_____

_____

_____

_____

_____

One of the greatest challenges that we face as teachers today is the predominance among students to play what I call the *blame game.* This behavior involves blaming all failure or confusion in the classroom on the teacher. This blame shifting is an easy way out of taking responsibility for performance issues in and out of the classroom. Holding students responsible for their behavior and performance demands that you, the teacher, communicate clearly your objectives and support those objectives with an organized and well-developed course. Try to find ways to show your students that they are the ones responsible for their education and that you, the teacher, are facilitating the process that is key to their success. This belief in student accountability will help you maintain your home for learning free from blame shifting and conflict.

This is why the *Art of Teaching* is so important to creating a home for learning that is truly functional. The next two chapters will explore the *Science of Teaching* and important skills such as creating objectives, communicating clearly and staying organized. With a perfect balance between both the *Art of Teaching* and the *Science of Teaching*, your home for learning will be *a heart-centered* and inspiring community of transformation!

"The mediocre teacher tells. The good teacher explains. The superior teacher demonstrates. The great teacher inspires."
- William Arthur Ward, British novelist

Chapter 3 - The Science of Teaching

"Prior proper planning prevents poor performance"
                                                -Anonymous

A long time ago, I heard the following phrase: "Prior proper planning prevents poor performance." While this phrase may seem like another witty saying, the content applies directly to student and teacher success in the classroom. With this phrase in mind, let's take a look at two family situations that relate to the *Science of Teaching*:

Situation 1

Family A (mother, father, and two children) in Wisconsin are leaving for vacation in a half-hour. Their destination: a long drive across the country to Bangor, Maine. Nothing is packed, not even a single item of clothing. Family A has not mentioned to anyone that they will be leaving for vacation, and that their house will be unattended for a week (neighbors do not know, neither do the local police nor Family A's local relatives). So, the chances that somebody will check on their house while they are on vacation are very slim.

Family A does not have any directions (even though they have never been to Maine before); they figured they could follow highway signs all the way to Maine. They also do not have any hotel reservations in Bangor, so where they stay is up in the air. Their five year-old car has not been serviced, so if the car's brakes or engine are in need of repair, Family A is taking a gamble. After all, who knows what could happen on a long drive across the country...

You may begin to think: this family does not seem ready to leave for vacation in a half-hour. What type of vacation could they possibly have? A restful one? Or perhaps they won't even make it out of Wisconsin!

Situation 2

Family B (mother, father, and two children) in Wisconsin are leaving for vacation in a half-hour. Their destination: a long drive across the country to Bangor, Maine. All of their belongings are packed from beach clothes to formal dinner attire, to traveler's checks and toothpaste. They told their family, who lives nearby, that they would be gone for seven days and asked them to check on their house while they are gone. Additionally, Family B gave their family the hotel name and phone number in Maine just in case they need to reach them. Further, not wanting to take any chances, Family B called their local police station, asking them to also check on their house while they are gone. Family B has detailed directions on how to get to Bangor and they are bringing those directions, along with relevant road atlases and maps along with them on their journey. They have confirmed their hotel reservation for their arrival the next day. To ensure a safe trip, their five year-old car was recently serviced by a trusted mechanic and was cleared for the trip. Family B is eating breakfast, talking with excitement about their upcoming family journey…

How ready do you think Family B is? They seem to have planned accordingly and are ready to go full steam ahead to Maine. Which vacation would you rather be a part of? Most likely, Family B, because they have planned prior to their departure and are ready for their journey across the country.

This analogy extends to the journey that takes place in the classroom as well: if you were a student, whose classroom would you rather be in? Teacher A, who is unorganized, chaotic in his/her mannerisms, and seems to lack clear goals for the classroom? Or, Teacher B, who is ready for class to begin, has class materials organized (handouts, resources, activities...), has the day's learning objective(s) written on the chalkboard along with the homework assignment for the next class session? More than likely, if you were a student, you would rather be in Teacher B's classroom. Why? Amongst other things, an organized teacher communicates learning objectives to the class, what the goal of the class session is, and discusses relevance of class material (i.e. in relation to the "real world"). These characteristics, and others which will be explained, are associated with the *Science of Teaching*.

> *"Good teaching is one-fourth preparation and three-fourths theater."*
>
> -Gail Godwin, American writer

Godwin's quote is profound as it proposes that planning and preparation is a necessary element in creating a home for learning. What benefits do you think students derive from organized, relevant, and well thought out instruction? Take a few moments and brainstorm

your top five answers:

1._____

_____

_____

_____

2._____

_____

_____

_____

3._____

_____

_____

_____

4._____

_____

_____

_____

5._____

_____

_____

_____

"Why Are We Doing This?" Making Learning Relevant

Our students benefit from organized educators in several ways. Primarily, students know what is expected from them and what the instructor will deliver to them in class sessions. Therefore, students can focus on lecture material, in-class activities, and apply this material to "real world" applications. Consequently, students can become actively involved in the class session, which can help in the retention and application of class material. Finally, by understanding expectations, students can better prepare themselves for exams, papers, projects, and/or other means of evaluation.

In order to nurture a home for learning, you need to cultivate an educational environment that helps students grow toward attaining their educational goals. By providing guidance through complex class material, structure through directions, and clarity of expectations, students can better focus on absorbing class material. On the other hand, an unorganized educator provides a chaotic environment for students, where students are left to guess what is expected of them, how they will be assessed, and why material is relevant. This guessing on the students' part can frustrate the student to the point of indifference, apathy, and possibly anger toward the educator or course material. Once a student experiences these negative emotions, a wedge has been driven between the student and educator. This wedge disrupts the home for learning and may eventually lead to a house of horrors for student and educator alike.

To nurture educational growth in the home for learning, teachers should understand the two elements to the *Science of Teaching*:

1. Planning the class session ahead of time;

2. Carrying out the class session plan (lesson plan) in class

Let's explore these two critical elements further, in order to understand how to plan and carry out an effective class session.

Creating Clear Objectives

Planning the class session ahead of time

The way to achieve success as an educator in class is to plan for success *prior* to class. Specifically, educators would benefit from planning their class sessions with five principles in mind:

- Relevance to students

- Discussing the relevant material

- Student performance done in class

- Environment/conditions for student performance

- Criteria for success

1. Making the goal of the class session relevant to your students

Relevance in this educational context can be defined as "a student perception of whether the course instruction/content satisfies personal needs, personal goals, and/or career goals" (Frymier & Shulman, 1995, pg. 42). Relevance is probably the most important reason why educators exist: to motivate students to want to absorb course material to learn how course material impacts their lives. Studies indicate that student interest in class material is increased when students see the relevance of class material, which may influence a positive attitude toward the class and instructor (Shaw & Young, 1999). Discussing how information will help students gain employment in their field of interest and how to achieve success on the job are ways to make material relevant to students. In short, teachers would benefit from linking class material to the relevant needs of their students. One simple way to determine how material would be relevant to a class is to ask yourself: 1) why should the students care about the class material? and, 2) how will their lives be positively influenced with knowing this class material?

2. Deciding how you will discuss the relevant class material

Once an educator knows how to make the course material relevant to the students, he/she would then need to further develop those ideas. Specifically, what would you say in your lecture to indicate relevance, and what activities or supporting material (i.e. quotes, testimony, statistics,...) would you rely on to increase retention through relevance?

Here are some approaches we have used that increases relevance to students:

- ask thought provoking questions ("do you think our book is right when it says...")

- use appropriate statistics ("ninety-five percent of employers say a good resume will help land an interview")

- cite quotes and testimony ("according to Fred Smith, Human Resources Manager, dressing appropriate for an interview is the first thing he notices in job candidates")

- bring in related newspaper and/or industry journal articles ("here is an article I found in last month's *The Daily News,* which discusses effective interviewing techniques")

One final, simple method of establishing relevance is to introduce the class session's topic at the beginning of class and then ask the class "why is this material important for us to know?" Invariably, these tactics will help engage the students' interest at the outset of class, providing for an attentive class audience.

3. Student performance in class

After the educator determines how to communicate relevance to the class, he/she will then plan strategies to aid retention and to apply critical class material. While there are some situations which may be a bit of a challenge to do small group work in class (lecture class of over 300 students may be challenging, but it can be done), educators should be encouraged to integrate some form of active participation into the class session, as opposed to students passively listening to a lecture for an extended amount of time. In other words, what will the students be doing in class to help them understand, retain, and apply class material? Planning student performance with action verbs in mind would be an invaluable step toward effectively organizing a class lecture.

Sample action verbs include: *achieve, build, conduct, diagnose, explain, forecast, generate, head up, inspect, monitor, negotiate, operate, present, repair, solve, translate, upgrade, validate,* and *write.*

Action verbs require students to do something; to be involved in the learning process, to analyze the material, and apply the material. This sort of active participation is beneficial to educators in several ways: 1) students personalize information; 2) students increase comprehension and retention through application of material; and, 3) after evaluating the student performance (and even during their performance, in some cases), instructors get immediate feedback on how well students comprehended the material. If students comprehended the material, then the class can move forward with the unit/lecture/activity. If students do not comprehend the material, then the instructor can spend some more time processing the difficult material with the students.

4. Environment/Conditions for student performance

It is not enough to know which activities or student participation methods you will use; instructors then need to brainstorm more specific aspects of the environment/conditions that the student performance is working within. Specifically:

- are students processing course material individually or with other students in small groups?

- if students are placed in groups, how many people are in the small groups (two, four, six, etc.)?

- is there a time limit for the student performance (ten minutes, half-hour, entire class session)?

- will students have access to resources (textbooks or notes) or will they be required to perform with their own knowledge?

- how will students know if they achieved success?

Providing students with specific environmental guidelines or conditions of success like these will allow them to focus on material and actively participate in the learning activity. Why? Because the material is relevant to them and the students know what is occurring in the relevant learning activity.

5. Criteria for student success

Once the student learning activity has been planned, the educator should determine how both the educator and students will know if the students achieved a level of success. In other words, the educator needs to know before the student learning activity begins, the level of student performance the students should achieve at the conclusion of the student learning activity. Clearly, this information is helpful for the educator and student, as it provides information necessary for planning how to evaluate the student performance in the learning activity.

Some methods of determining criteria is to set time limits (complete the learning activity within a certain time…), percentage points or number of permissible errors allowed (…with 85% success, including no more than five grammatical errors). Naturally, educators can combine these criteria, add, delete, or modify them for additional evaluation purposes.

While this five-step planning process may seem complex, perhaps an applied example of planning a class session would help in understanding this process.

An educator has a fifty-minute *Fundamentals of Job Searching* class tomorrow at 3:00 pm and needs to formulate a class lesson plan. The goal of the class session is to introduce different resume formats and have students understand when to use the different formats.

1. **Making the goal of the class session relevant to your students**

At the very beginning of the class session, the educator would ask the students: "How many of you have a resume that could get you a job in your field today? How many of you would like to have such a resume?" By planning on asking thought provoking questions, the educator can grab the students' attention because they are interested in obtaining employment after graduation. Students may wonder *how ready am I for my job search? Gee, I better get my resume in order!* (5 minutes)

2. Discussing the relevant material further

After asking the relevant and thought provoking questions, the educator would then plan on incorporating statistics on what employers look for in resumes, he/she could use handouts from newspapers and job search websites which quote Human Resource professionals on what a good resume entails. Additionally, the educator could then distribute sample resumes, which could be referred to as *archetypal resumes* because these resumes should be used as the guides on what an effective resume is. In other words, these archetypal resumes would be distributed to the students to show them exactly what a good resume looks like. After distributing these resumes (chronological, functional, and skills resumes), the educator would highlight the similarities and differences among the different formats, and would ask the students which situations would call for the different resumes.

After walking the students through the different resume formats, the students can begin to apply what they learned to themselves-*which resume would be good for me and when should I use it?* As the student pays attention to the information, these questions should be answered shortly (8 minutes).

3. Student performance done in class

The educator would then plan on distributing and reviewing mock resumes, from poorly developed to well developed, in the different resume formats. The educator would want the students to evaluate the effectiveness of these mock resumes based on the information they obtained in #2. Here the educator allows the students to actively apply what they just learned about resume formats, in order to evaluate sample resumes. This sort of critical evaluation is helpful as students begin to understand which resume format would be good for them to use.

4. Environment/Conditions for student performance

The educator will explain that students will work individually and can use the archetypal resumes when they evaluate the mock resumes. Students will have twenty-five minutes to evaluate all seven of the mock resumes (3 minutes for explanation).

5. Criteria for evaluation

Again, students have twenty-five minutes to evaluate the seven mock resumes, but have to highlight and correct 90% of the errors on each of the seven mock resumes. Students will find out the correct answers at the end of the twenty-five minutes as the educator will read off the errors and discuss how to correct these errors (30 minutes for activity and review of activity).

These last two steps of the educator's class session plan will help the students see what good resumes are, how to correct bad resumes, and to better understand when to use the different resumes formats.

Once the educator writes down all of these plans prior to class, the end result is a lesson plan, a plan which guides the material and student/educator actions in the upcoming class session. To add to this lesson plan, an effective educator could add an optional sixth step: wrap up and discuss the next class's assignment (4 minutes).

Staying Organized

Carrying out the class session

The educator can now walk into the classroom ready to conduct a class session worthy of being in the home for learning. However, knowing the elements of your lesson plan prior to the start of the class session is half the battle of the *Science of Teaching*. Successfully carrying out the lesson plan in class makes up the other half of the *Science of Teaching*. There are six steps to this in class process of carrying out the material, and we can refer to this process as the "Six-Step Class Session Process." This six-step process is as follows:

1. **Communicating objectives of the class session to the students**
2. **Establishing immediate relevance to students**
3. **Facilitating discussion and relevance of new class material**
4. **Processing student performance activity (with criteria for success)**

5. Debriefing the student performance activity

6. Formally evaluating student retention of material

To help understand this process, let's take a look at a few of the behaviors that accompany these steps before we look at an applied example:

1. **Communicating objectives of the class session to the students**

    - List learning objectives on the chalkboard

    - Preview these learning objectives at the beginning of class;

2. **Establishing immediate relevance to students**

    - Relate learning objectives/material to students and their needs

    - Incorporate statistics and/or supporting material which reinforces the importance of the objectives/material;

3. **Facilitating discussion and relevance of new class material**

    - Present new information that would enhance student knowledge of the objectives/material

- Ask thought-provoking questions which encourage students to think about the objectives/material;

4. **Processing student performance activity (with criteria for success)**

   - Provide instruction to the class on what type of learning activity will be used to apply the material (small group work vs. individual work)

   - Give class specific guidelines on what they are to achieve in the performance activity;

5. **Debriefing the student performance activity**

   - Ask students to share their feelings about what they learned in the student performance activity

   - Highlight what the students may have missed when summing up the valuable aspects of the activity; and

6. **Formally evaluating student retention of material**

   - Assess student knowledge/retention of the material via papers, exams, quizzes, projects, etc.

   - This assessment provides both the teacher and the student a barometer for how the student retained the material

Now, let's look at these steps a little more in depth, while applying the resume lesson plan we previously discussed. In other words, we will examine how we can place the resume lesson plan into an actual class session.

Communicating Objectives Clearly

1. **Communicating objectives of the class session to the students**

Prior to the start of class (five to ten minutes or so) the educator should write up in one of the corners of the chalkboard what objectives will be covered that day and what the homework is for the next class session. Our previous job search class example could be written as follows: *Objectives of the Day* 1) Discuss the importance of resumes, 2) Analyze different resume formats, and 3) Evaluate mock resumes. Assignment for next time: Quiz on resume formats, and read Chapter 2 on Interviewing.

As students walk into the classroom and sit down in their seats, the educator can now turn his/her attention to greeting and welcoming the students. This greeting activity prior to class is helpful in nurturing the growth of the students in the home for learning. As class begins, the educator says: "Good afternoon, folks. How is everybody today? Good? Good. Today we are going to discuss the importance of a well-constructed resume, and analyze different resume formats. Before we begin, are there any questions from last time?"

After greeting the students and previewing the class session objectives, a friendly yet organized tone is set for the class session. The students understand the goal of the class session and have an idea of what is to be covered over the next fifty-minutes.

2. Establishing immediate relevance to the students

This step calls the instructor to directly relate the class session material to the audience in terms of how they can benefit from the material.

- Ask thought provoking questions ("How many of you have a resume that could get you a job in your field today? How many of you would like to have such a resume?")

- Discuss statistics on how "ninety-five percent of human resource professionals say a good resume will help land a job interview."

- Distribute newspaper article regarding job search tips, saying "Here is an article I found in last month's *The Daily News* which discusses effective job search strategies. Among the top recommendations: a well constructed resume"

- The educator would then say: "Clearly, it seems as though a well constructed resume is the first step toward professional success in today's economy. What do you think?"

After absorbing this information, students cannot help but be interested in how to construct and analyze effective resumes. Why? They want to get a job after graduation, and the educator's supporting material indicated an effective resume is helpful in achieving that goal.

"A good teacher, like a good entertainer, first must hold his audience's attention. Then he can teach his lesson."
-Hendrick John Clarke, American poet and editor

3. Facilitating discussion and relevance of new class material

This step would present new information which would enhance student understanding of the material (distributing the three archetypal resumes and highlighting which situations warrant their use). Further, the educator could refer to material discussed in previous class sessions and how they interrelate. For example, the educator could say: "Last week we explored our soft skills, technical skills, and the professional skills we obtained from our previous work experience. Now we will transfer those skills and strengths onto our resumes." Further, the educator could ask yet again a thought provoking question: "After looking at these three resume formats, which format do you think would be most relevant to you and why?"

By exploring the new material and making its relevance known, educators bring to life the relevance of the class session. Students can benefit almost immediately from this new information.

4. Processing student performance activity with criteria for success

After discussing new class material and its relevance, the educator may then proceed with an in-class learning activity. This step is critical because it:

- Increases retention of new material through practice

- Allows students to personalize information (they may then think *So this is how I am going to apply this!*)

Referring back to our job search class lesson plan in the previous section, let's examine how the educator would carry out Step 4:

"You will work individually and can use the archetypal resumes when you evaluate the mock resumes. You will have twenty-five minutes to evaluate all seven of the mock resumes. Additionally, you will have to highlight and correct 90% of the errors on each of the seven mock resumes. After the twenty-five minutes are up, we will share our answers and compare them to what I have as being correct."

Through practice, students can better grasp the new information. Further, students can make the material then relevant to their educational growth (*Which resume works best for me? Ah, yes! The functional resume!*).

5. Debriefing the student performance activity

After the student performance activity is completed and processed, the educator would then tie the loose, yet necessary, ends together:

- Highlight what the students learned in the student performance activity ("Today we looked at which situations warrant different resumes, how to construct and analyze the different resume formats, and what not to do on a resume.")

- Highlight what the students may have missed in the student performance activity ("One thing I would like to point out, which did not come up in our discussion today, is that you never include your references on the same page as your resume. Your references should be on a separate sheet.")

- Play Devil's Advocate or turn the tables on the students ("What if you sent out ten resumes to employers and did not receive a response? What would you do then?")

Debriefing can raise student awareness of the complexity of the new material and encourage them to reflect on the material after class. Additionally, educators can bring in new insights or other supporting material (newspaper articles, testimony from credible sources...) to reinforce student retention.

6. Formally evaluating retention of material

Students may forget material over time, so formal evaluation is necessary in order to reinforce what is the most relevant material. Formal evaluation of new material can be in the form of quizzes, exams, projects, papers, and reports. Our job search educator can preview his/her next class by telling them they are in for a formal evaluation of their retention: "Next class session, you will have to correct a functional, chronological, and skills resume, without notes, for a quiz grade."

Not only does formal evaluation reinforce new material, it assesses students' learning of the new material. Then, both the educator and the student can measure the level of individual student retention. If retention is good, with the majority of students earning an 'A' or 'B' on the quiz, then the educator can feel confident in moving on to the next unit of instruction. If retention is not so good, with too many 'D's' or 'F's', perhaps the educator could intervene and ask the struggling students "what happened?" or could take a class session to review material again.

In order to achieve success in the classroom, an educator needs to plan ahead by organizing and developing relevant lesson plans prior to class. This information can provide a solid foundation from which the educator could conduct a successful class session and may provide a backup plan should the lesson not go as planned. Further, the educator can effectively carry out the lesson plan via the six-step class session process. This six-step class session process encourages effective delivery of the new material, since it maintains student interest through relevance and organization.

Conclusion

Think about it: which vacation would you rather go on? A planned vacation, or a hastily thrown together vacation? If you were a student, which class would you rather be a part of? A planned class, or a hastily thrown together class?

Think for a few moments about a class session you need to plan out. Use the five principles of lesson plans to brainstorm a lesson plan and then develop your six-step class session process to ensure a smooth delivery of material in the class session.

Lesson Plan

Relevance to students

_____

_____

_____

Discussing the relevant material

_____

_____

_____

Student performance done in class

_____

_____

_____

Environment/Conditions for student performance

_____

_____

_____

Criteria for success

_____

_____

_____

Optional wrap-up and preview next class session

_____

_____

_____

Six-Step Class Session Process

Communicating objectives of the class session

_____

_____

_____

Establishing immediate relevance to students

_____

_____

_____

Facilitating discussion and relevance of new class material

_____

_____

_____

Processing the student performance activity

_____

_____

_____

Debriefing the student performance activity

_____

_____

_____

Formally evaluating retention of new material

_____

_____

_____

Chapter 4 - Getting To Know Your Family

"We should honor our teachers more than our parents, because while our parents cause us to live, our teachers cause us to live well."

-Philoxenus, Greek poet

There is a lot of literature circulating around about effective parenting techniques. If you read the diverse body of parenting literature, some of the terms and specific language of the terms may change, but the main messages remain consistent: provide a loving, disciplined, emotionally stable environment which contributes to the mental and physical well-being of the child. This approach would help a child grow into a well-rounded individual, one who knows right from wrong, understands and practices respect, appreciates hard work, and is respectful in relationships.

So, in the early years, children are nurtured by their parents or immediate family. Then around the age of four or five, children begin attending school, and very well could spend the majority of the next fifteen to twenty years of their lives in educational settings. Fifteen to twenty years is a long time, considering that the majority of those years are spent emotionally, intellectually, spiritually, and physically growing toward responsible adulthood. Parents do a wonderful job of raising their children, and educators also do an excellent job of shaping the children, young adults, and college-aged students into responsible adults. An educator's role in developing students is awesome, and should not be taken lightly.

> *"A teacher affects eternity; he can never tell where his influence stops."*
>
> - Henry Brooks Adams, American historian

With this great duty of developing students, educators must not only practice *The Art and Science of Teaching*, but also embody the qualities associated with good parenting techniques: provide a loving, disciplined, emotionally stable environment which contributes to the mental and physical well-being of the students. *Viewing and interacting with students in this family-oriented, heart-centered, approach clearly fosters a home-like environment in the classroom.* Indeed, a home for learning is then born.

Creating A Personality Picture

I once overheard a father talking to a new parent about the joys and struggles of parenthood. The one thing that the experienced father, a proud father of two boys, kept reiterating was how his two sons were completely different, and how important it was for him to understand that in order to be an effective parent, he needed to treat his sons differently. In doing so, the experienced father would still provide a disciplined and caring environment. However, it was just the means of delivering this environment that was different. For example, the oldest son, when he got out of line, could be talked to in a straightforward, blunt manner. He seemed to respond positively to this approach. The youngest, however, would get his feelings hurt and "melt," so a different, softer approach had to be used (even though the message may be the same). Both boys are now grown, living responsible and contented lives.

You may have heard of the following sayings, which serve as philosophies for some people:

Golden Rule: "Do unto others as you would have done unto you."

Platinum Rule: "Treat others as they want to be treated."

While these approaches are fine and are appropriate in certain contexts, it should be noted that a new philosophy should be adopted for the educational setting. This philosophy would nurture and develop a home for learning.

"Treat others (students) as they need to be treated and how they want to be treated."

To be successful in the classroom, what do you think students need?

_____

_____

_____

_____

_____

Probably coming up with your list of student needs was not extremely difficult. Some needs you may have recorded: respect, relevant material, fair instructor, challenging assignments or projects, caring instructor, and so on. However, how students want these needs delivered in the educational setting varies from student to student and class to class. Just like children respond to and need different parenting techniques, students respond to and need different educational approaches in the classroom. Some students like passive educational settings while others thrive in hands-on settings; some like the educator using examples and demonstrations to make the lecture material relevant and comprehensible.

So how do educators know what students want? We simply ask them. By asking students what they want, educators can get a feel for educational approaches that would work for the class. Additionally, educators would begin to get a picture of the class personality as a whole, and individual student personalities within the classroom. An easy way to ask what students need, in order to be successful learners in the classroom, is to address this question on the first day of class, or if in a corporate training session, within the first half-hour or hour (depending on how long the training session is: two hours versus four hours versus eight hours). Educators could ask the following questions, which will help the educator better understood the needs of the class:

- What do you want to get out of this class (or training session)-skills, competencies, etc.,?

- What do you expect of me as the professor/instructor/teacher/trainer? And/Or, how would you like me to treat you?

- What should I expect from you, to help you achieve your goals in this class (goals determined from question #1)

Recording these responses on the chalkboard or poster-board and holding everyone in the class, including yourself, accountable throughout the duration of the class is advised. Further, a constructive dialogue about class expectations have begun, and student awareness and interest in course content has been piqued.

Asking these questions is a powerful tool for breaking down tensions and student stress levels while building a home for learning. Why? When educators are concerned about the student responses (i.e. student needs), the students then begin to see the educator as someone who genuinely cares about them and their success in the classroom.

"Everywhere, we learn from those we love."
- Johann Wolfgang Von Goethe, German poet and dramatist

Teaching with the students' needs in mind will bring respect, caring, and perhaps love into the home for learning.

"Students Are A lot Like People!"

Remember, as odd as it may sound, *students are a lot like people!* Just like you, your family, your friends, and the authors of this book, students have needs. These needs should always be in the forefront of an educator's mind as soon as he/she walks into the classroom. Think about it: if your child were sick, in order to know how to remedy his/her problems, you would first try to determine what is wrong or what hurts them. Essentially, you are conducting a needs assessment when you ask the sick child what hurts them. Do they feel nauseous? Do they have the chills? After knowing what the child's needs are, you can deliver appropriate remedies *to satisfy those needs.* This same principle holds true in the classroom. An educator should ask the students what their educational needs are on the first day of class, and then devote the remaining class sessions to solving those relevant educational needs as long as those needs are relevant to what is being taught in the class and consistent with the course's learning objectives.

Using Various Personality Sorters

One tool we recommend teachers use to understand individual student personality needs is to have students take valid personality tests. Myers-Briggs offers many different types of tests, and having the student participate in these instruments are fun and educational. When my colleague and I perform faculty training, we use Myers-Briggs as an assessment tool to better understand faculty, and then relate their test results to the teaching techniques that can benefit their personality style. Further, in the training sessions, we discuss personality styles as they relate to students and student learning behavior and needs. In sum, we match all of the personality styles of faculty to their teaching styles and then to the different student personality/learning styles and needs. With this information, educators can deliver material and messages that are relevant to the student needs.

Another method educators could use to identify student needs is to determine specifically how students process information. From our combined thirty years of teaching experience, we have noticed different ways students prefer to process information. Further, our insights are consistent with modern literature on student learning styles (see Nicholl and Rose, 1997). Are students visual learners, auditory learners, or kinesthetic learners? Understanding the characteristics of these three learning styles can aid in a more relevant approach to students in the home for learning.

From our experiences, the different learning styles respond to the following teaching mehods:

Characteristics of Visual Learners

- May like to see demonstrations, charts, diagrams, slides, educational videos to reinforce new material

- May expect clearly defined instructions and their lecture notes are very in-depth (probably would benefit from the educator writing key information on the chalk-board or highlighted in a power-point presentation)

- May sit at the front of the classroom, to get a clear vision of the educator, chalk-board, and other supplemental resources

- May lose focus by disorganization and erratic movements

In short, visual learners process information through *seeing*. What other educational strategies could you use to present information to visual learners?

_____

_____

_____

_____

How else could you tell if a student was a visual learner?

_____

_____

_____

_____

Characteristics of Auditory Learners

- May like to have spoken instructions or detailed explanations in addition to written directions

- To comprehend new material, may benefit from group activities which process complex information

- May pay attention to not only what the educator and classmates say, but may also seek meaning in how words are said (tone of voice)

- May lose focus if unusual noises and sounds occur in the classroom (for example, side conversations of fellow classmates, sirens outside the window...)

In short, auditory learners process information through *listening*. What other educational strategies could you use to present information to auditory learners?

_____

_____

_____

_____

How else could you tell if a student was an auditory learner?

_____

_____

_____

_____

Characteristics of Kinesthetic Learners

- May be very hands on and like to jump right in and try new things (learn through experience)

- May lose focus if sitting for long periods of time (i.e. long lecture sessions without any breaks or activities)

- May get antsy and *need* to do an in-class activity to remain focused on material and process information

In short, kinesthetic learners process information through *doing*-moving around or staying active, and/or even performing a hands-on demonstration of the material. What other educational strategies could you use to present information to kinesthetic learners?

_____

_____

_____

How else could you tell if a student was a kinesthetic learner?

_____

_____

_____

Understanding student personality and learning styles can help educators deliver relevant information via appropriate mediums of delivery. Respecting the different learning and personality styles can be beneficial for students and educator alike as students feel understood, encouraged, and free to learn without limitations. As an educator, could you ask for anything else in the minds of your students in your home for learning?

Conclusion

In conclusion, adapting a compassionate and understanding viewpoint toward your students, like you would your own family, is key to fostering a home for learning. When students feel the educator is genuine, loyal, and concerned about their needs and goals, students feel more comfortable in the classroom and have a positive view of the educator and course material. Further, positive nonverbals, like smiling, reinforcing head-nods, and addressing students by their name can help the different student personalities and learning styles relax and become involved in the course material, which could enhance their retention of information.

The experienced parent understands and responds to different child needs in his/her family. The experienced educator understands and responds to different student needs in their educational family.

Take a few moments and think about how you can better get to know your student family. What particular strategies could you use to better understand your students' educational needs? In other words, what activities, personality tests, or questions could you ask to better understand how your students learn and process information?

_____

_____

_____

Further, think for a few moments about difficult students you have had in the past. What strategies could you employ to help positively assimilate them back into the home for learning?

_____

_____

_____

Chapter 5 - Closing Thoughts: Moving Toward a New Philosophy of Teaching, *A Home for Learning*

"The ideal condition would be, I admit, that men should be right by instinct; but since we are all likely to go astray, the reasonable thing is to learn from those who can teach."
                                                -Sophocles, Greek dramatist

The journey toward a home for learning begins in the teacher's heart and is carried out in his/her actions in the classroom. While this book explores a number of tips to achieve educational effectiveness, we must now move toward practicing the advice contained in these pages. Throughout this book, we explored a *heart-centered philosophy* of teaching which views the students as family and the classroom as a family environment. Further, *the Art of Teaching* seeks to bring out the best in students by projecting a caring, respectful, and understanding attitude. This attitude will cultivate a home for learning, one that is positive for the students to learn in and the educator to teach in.

While understanding your students and respecting their needs are essential to creating a home for learning, it is really only half of the equation. Planning and carrying out a relevant class session is the second half of the equation: the *Science of Teaching*. A well-planned and executed class session can create and maintain student interest, while helping the student grasp vital information.

Thus, the *Art and Science of Teaching* leaves nothing to chance, plans for success, and respects the students as one would respect his/her family. Additionally, creating a home for learning takes a special approach and requires a noble attitude. Creating a home for learning lies in the educator's classroom philosophy, view of students, view of difficult situations, and organizational skills. Let's break these four items down for practical use:

To create a home for learning, adopt the following *classroom philosophy*:

- the classroom is a home, where the educator provides a structured and caring learning environment
- students are worthy of the respect we would show our family members. Understanding their needs, fears, goals, and career aspirations will help cultivate a positive learning environment
- classes should be fun, interactive, and allow students to think critically

To create a home for learning, adopt the following *view of students*:

- students are to be treated with respect, caring, and understanding

- students can add to the learning environment by sharing their insights, thoughts, and experiences

- students have the right to be intellectually challenged and taught with their needs in mind

To create a home for learning, adopt the following *view of difficult situations*:

- even the best class session planning and execution cannot prevent *some* problems from arising. Problems should be viewed as a learning opportunity so the problem does not happen again

- approach difficult situations with an open mind; remain positive while seeking the input from others, by asking questions (for example, "how can we get through this?")

- when confronting a student regarding his/her disruptive behavior, the educator does so in private, focuses on his/her disruptive behavior, instead of a personal attack, and how his/her behavior harms his/her learning process and possibly how the behavior harms the learning process of his/her classmates

To create a home for learning, adopt the following *organizational skills*:

- plan (ahead of time) relevant class sessions, including material and activities
- when planning class sessions, be mindful of possible student responses and/or questions; be prepared for those responses and/or questions
- at the beginning of the class session, preview the key points of the class session; at the end of the class session, review key material and insights, and briefly preview the next class session-what chapters/material will be covered, what the homework is…

After reading and practicing the information in this book, you can begin your journey toward teaching effectiveness. You will find that you have had the necessary abilities to achieve success in the classroom all along. Be patient with yourself and your students, and adhere to this *heart-centered approach*, for in time you will reap the rewards of cultivating a home for learning!

Good luck!!

So are you still skeptical about the importance of this *heart-centered approach*? Reflect on the following example, based on a true story, from one of the authors, Jim Slouffman:

I am reminded of a true story that best reflects the powerful impact that a home for learning can have on a student's life. I once had in my home for learning a student named Tommy. Tommy came from a very disadvantaged background. He grew up in what could be effectively called a war zone. Poverty was the norm and gang warfare was commonplace. Tommy's older brother was killed in a gun battle when he was just a teenager. This greatly embittered Tommy and his entire family. Tommy came to our college with a bit of a chip on his shoulder but the sincere desire to make a change in his life that just might change his future. By now he had three children of his own and was happily married. He came to us full of hope and ready to work.

Tommy's reaction to our functional home for learning was miraculous! (Miracle 1: event that cannot be explained by known laws of nature - Miraculous 2: marvel) Tommy made friends that were true and long lasting. He would come alive in class and shine with such joy that it would light up the whole room with warmth. He had finally found a sanctuary in which to grow to his full potential. As our little family of students bonded and became closer, Tommy would talk about his past and how it had dominated his future drive for success. Tommy wanted a fresh start, one that would be positive and rewarding for him and his family. We all agreed that the hope we all shared for a new life after graduation would become a reality through hard work, focus, and being supportive of our collective vision.

By and by graduation day finally arrived and how we all shared in this great accomplishment. Hand shakes, hugs and faces full of smiles best told the story of what this day meant to Tommy and his family. Everyone was delighted with what we had collectively accomplished. Though we all felt great joy, we were also saddened as we had to part and go our separate ways. It was kind of like saying good-bye to close family members at the airport before they leave for the gate. You know that you will hopefully see them again but realize it may involve a long period of time before such a reunion. Such is the closeness engendered in the home for learning.

Time passed since last we said good-bye to Tommy. He and a partner had started their own successful business. Prosperity had come to his home and his family was doing well. Tommy would come down to the college for a short visit from time to time. I noticed that he always brought his children with him. We would chat and discuss his success and what a great time we had in our home for learning. His respect for the college and what it had helped him accomplish was always evident in our conversations. It was for me a validation of what a *heart-centered approach* to teaching can accomplish.

Several more months had passed and we had not heard from Tommy. We all just assumed that he was busy with his career and did not have the time to stop by. Then came the tragic news that Tommy had been killed in a gang-related crime. We were all deeply touched by Tommy's death; we could not bear to think about his young, wonderful life being cut short. We were lost in an abyss of sad questions: could we have done more to help Tommy and his family? What can we do now to help his family? The answers came in the form of a phone call. It was Tommy's family. They had gotten together to somehow find a way to pay tribute to Tommy's tragic but important life. They called us to gain permission to etch the college's logo upon his gravestone. They told us very sincerely that Tommy had constantly reminded them that his years at the college were the best years of his entire life. Tommy's family wanted his wonderful memories of the college to be memorialized along with Tommy at his final resting spot...

And so now you can see the meaning and importance of creating a home for learning in your classroom. It is not just an attitude or technique. It is a powerful form of life transformation. Be empowered with a *heart-centered approach* to teaching and let your home for learning be filled with compassion. You and your students deserve it!

"To me the sole hope of human salvation lies in teaching."
-George Bernard Shaw, Irish dramatist

In order to continue our dialogue with you, our fellow educators, please contact us via our website www.educationtrainingassociates.com

Workbook Exercises For Educators

TEACHING SUCCESS ACTION PLAN

Think for a few moments about the *heart-centered* approach to teaching and the *Art and Science* of teaching. What are some things you should 1) start doing; 2) stop doing; and 3) continue doing to create the home for learning you desire in your classroom?

START DOING?   BY WHEN?
-
-
-
-

STOP DOING?   BY WHEN?
-
-
-
-

CONTINUE DOING?   BY WHEN?
-
-
-
-

NOTES FOR TEACHING SUCCESS ACTION PLAN

PERSONAL REFLECTION

Take a few moments and reflect on the following items:

1. What are some actions/behaviors that *I currently do* that support a home for learning? How, specifically, do these actions support a home for learning?

2. What are some actions/behaviors *I need to currently do* to support a home for learning? How can I go about achieving these actions/behaviors (i.e. what resources will help me?) and by when should I expect to achieve these aspirations?

3. What are some actions/behaviors *I currently do which may discourage a home for learning*? How can I reduce these actions/behaviors?

Ryan Hall and Jim Slouffman

NOTES FOR PERSONAL REFLECTION

References

Frymier, A., and Shulman, G. (1995). "What's in it for me?": Increasing content relevance to enhance student's motivation. Communication Education, 44, pps. 40-50.

Kelly-Gangi, Carol, and Jude Patterson. *The Gift Of Teaching: A Book of Favorite Quotations To Inspire and Encourage*. New York: Barnes and Noble Books, 2002.

Nicholl, Malcolm. J., and Rose, Colin. *Accelerated Learning For The 21st Century: The Six-Step Plan To Unlock Your Master-Mind*. New York: Delacorte Press, 1997

Ricard, M. and Trinh, T.X. *The Quantum And The Lotus*. Crown Publishers, New York, 2001

Shaw, D. and Young, S. (1999). Profiles of effective college and university teachers. <u>The Journal of Higher Education</u>, 70, pps. 670-685.

"The root of mankind is the family."
-Blessed Adolph Kolping, Social philospher

Student, Faculty and Staff Testimonials

"We learn much more than how to make attractive and effective art work at Antonelli, because of the instructors' compassion for what we are striving to become. Encouragement and support never go unnoticed."
        - Kim Shaw, Student

"Knowledge is the most essential part of modern living. A teacher's job is to let us have this knowledge and Jim does this wonderfully. Not because he assigns projects or gives us tests, but because of the creative freedom he provides."
        - Clayton Beeney, Student

"I will always cherish and hold in my heart the day one of my students handed me a package and the writing on the wrapping paper said 'thank you for being there for me not only as a teacher, but a friend. You have opened yourself up and gave a bit of yourself to all of us.' Inside the package was a book of quotes for teachers. The writing on the wrapping paper meant more to me than the present itself. To know that I have touched someone's life and passed my knowledge along to them for their future use is more rewarding to me than anything on earth."
        - Teresa Meyer, Teacher

"Well, I have worked for the last fifteen years in financial aid, twelve of those years at another institution. I have always felt as though my co-workers were my second family and was a little nervous about leaving my "family" of twelve years to move to a new one. My experience has been that not only did my new

"family" welcome me with open arms but the corporate staff is also part of the family here at Antonelli."

Leah C. Elkins, Financial Aid Administrator

"I love this school. I don't know if I could have made it somewhere else. The atmosphere here is one of a kind and really makes you feel special. I know I can go to any of my teachers if I have a problem. I would not trade my experiences here for anything in the world."

- Rachel Valetta, Student

"Public Speaking is one of the tougher courses I've taken in school (previous/high school). Mr. Hall has a way of making everyone comfortable in his class. I've learned a lot in this class and enjoyed having Mr. Hall as a teacher."

- Gina Kiep, Student

About The Authors

Jim Slouffman, Educator, Artist and Philosopher

Jim is the Director of Education and Department Chairman of Commercial Art at Antonelli College in Cincinnati, Ohio. He has an MFA from The College of DAAP, University of Cincinnati and a BFA from Wright State University. Jim has taught at the college level for thirty years and for twenty-five of those years at Antonelli College. He has also held teaching positions at The Art Academy of Cincinnati, College of Mt. Saint Joseph and Northern Kentucky University. In his current position, he is responsible for faculty and curriculum development as well as teaching full-time.

As a former member of both the NATTS (National Association of Trade and Technical Schools) and CCA (Career College Association) Professional Development Committees, he has been involved in many training activities nationwide. These activities included the Competency Based Staff Development Program and Education Managers Workshop. He was also past Chairman of the Editorial Review Board for *Classroom Companion*, a quarterly publication for career college teachers. He received the prestigious national "Teacher of the Year" award in 1993, presented by the Career College Association of Washington DC.

Ryan Hall, Educator and Corporate Trainer

Ryan is the Professional Development Coordinator and Department Chairman of Academics at Antonelli College in Cincinnati, Ohio. In addition to studying human resource management, he has an M.A. and B.A. in Organizational Communication from Miami University (Ohio). As a graduate student at Miami University, he taught in the Communication Department for two years and served on the Graduate Recruitment Committee. Before arriving at Antonelli College, he worked in the management consulting industry, researching and facilitating management development seminars for clients across the United States. He has facilitated workshops on: conflict management, leadership, change management, coaching skills, team-building, sexual harassment, and participative management.

In his current position at Antonelli College, he researches and conducts faculty and staff training workshops, provides orientation for new faculty members, oversees the development of the Academics Department, and teaches full-time in the Academics Department.